Oxford Read and Discover

Discover! 2

Sunny And Rainy

Louise Spilsbury

Contents

OXFORD
UNIVERSITY PRESS

OXFORD
UNIVERSITY PRESS

Great Clarendon Street, Oxford, OX2 6DP, United Kingdom

Oxford University Press is a department of the University of Oxford. It furthers the University's objective of excellence in research, scholarship, and education by publishing worldwide. Oxford is a registered trade mark of Oxford University Press in the UK and in certain other countries

ISBN: 978 0 19 464680 2

An Audio CD Pack containing this book and a CD is also available, ISBN 978 0 19 464690 1

The CD has a choice of American and British English recordings of the complete text.

An accompanying Activity Book is also available, ISBN 978 0 19 464670 3

Printed in China

This book is printed on paper from certified and well-managed sources.

ACKNOWLEDGEMENTS

Illustrations by: Kelly Kennedy pp.4, 7, 9, 12, 14, 15, 16, 23, 28; Alan Rowe pp.20, 21, 22, 25, 26, 27, 29, 30, 32, 33, 35, 38, 39.

The Publishers would also like to thank the following for their kind permission to reproduce photographs and other copyright material: Alamy pp.3 (rainy day/Spice Coast Collection/Balan Madhavan), 6 (zebras/McPHOTO/vario images GmbH & Co KG), 13 (flags/Pictor International/ImageState), 19 (umbrellas/ Fraser Band); Corbis pp.6 (rain/Michael S. Yamashita); Getty Images pp.8 (Ryan/Beyer), 9 (Seth Resnick/Science Faction), 10 (picturegarden/The Image Bank), 11 (skiing/Ashley Jouhar/ The Image Bank, snow in street/Stephen St. John/National Geographic), 18 (beach/Don Smith/Flickr), 19 (rain on roof/ Christopher Pillitz/The Image Bank); Naturepl.com p.17 (Doug Allan); Oxford University Press pp.3 (sunny day), 4, 15, 16, 18 (shutters); Photolibrary pp.14 (Luiz C Marigo/Peter Arnold Images); Science Photo Library pp.5 (Larry Landolfi), 13 (hurricane/Jim Edds).

 # Introduction

Can you see the sun in the sky?
Can you see rain? Is it sunny outside,
or is it rainy? What is your favorite
type of weather?

What do you do when it's sunny?
Do you like rainy weather?
What types of weather do you know?

 Now read and discover more
about the weather!

1 Sunny

sun

Earth

The sun is a star. It's very, very hot! The sun has lots of heat and light. Heat and light from the sun come to Earth. The heat and light make Earth warm so we can live here.

Discover!

Light from the sun comes to Earth in eight minutes!

Some places are warm and sunny all year, and they have no seasons. Some places have seasons. In summer, there's more light from the sun, so it's warm. In winter, there's less light from the sun, so it's cold.

Is it warm and sunny where you live?

In Summer

In Winter

→ Go to pages 20–21 for activities.

cloud

rain

Rain falls from clouds in the sky. There are many raindrops in a cloud. When small raindrops meet, they make one big raindrop. When there are lots of big raindrops, rain falls to Earth.

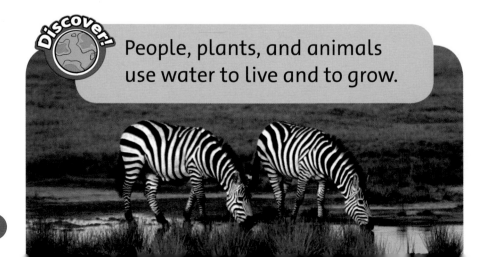

Discover!

People, plants, and animals use water to live and to grow.

When rain falls, water goes into rivers. Water in rivers goes into oceans. When it's sunny, water at the top of the ocean gets warm. Some of the water goes up into the sky. Water in the sky makes clouds. Then rain falls again! This is called the water cycle.

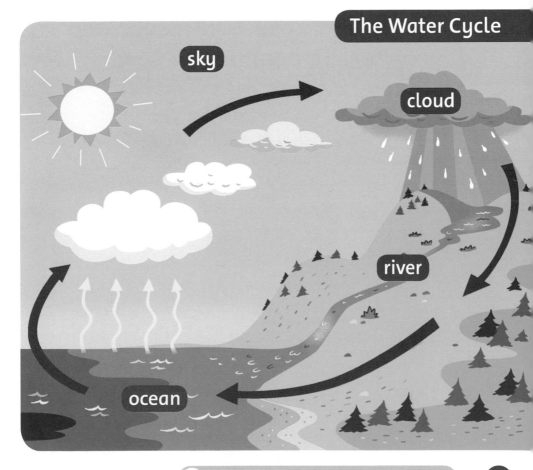

The Water Cycle

sky

cloud

river

ocean

Go to pages 22–23 for activities.

3 Cloudy

Do you see clouds in the sky where you live? Some clouds are gray and some clouds are white. Gray clouds have many raindrops. White clouds don't have many raindrops.

When it's cloudy, big clouds stop some light from the sun coming to Earth.

Cumulonimbus Clouds

Cumulonimbus clouds are very, very big. When you see this type of cloud, get your umbrella! Cumulonimbus clouds have lots and lots of raindrops, and they make very big storms.

Discover!

Cumulonimbus clouds can make lightning. Lightning is very, very hot!

lightning

→ Go to pages 24–25 for activities.

4 Snowy

When it's very cold in the sky, water in clouds is ice. Some ice falls to Earth. When it falls, the ice is snow. When snow falls on warm ground, the snow melts. Then the snow is water again. Some water goes into the ground and it helps plants to grow. Some water goes into rivers.

Snow Melting

Skiing on a Mountain

When snow falls on cold ground, it's white everywhere! When lots of snow falls on mountains, people can go skiing. When lots of snow falls on houses and streets, people can't drive their cars. Then they can't go to school or work.

Snow in a Street

Go to pages 26–27 for activities.

 Windy

Do you know the sun makes wind?

Wind is air that moves. In the sky there's air. The sun makes the air warm. Warm air goes up into the sky. In the sky it's very cold, so the air gets cold. When the air is cold, it goes down again.

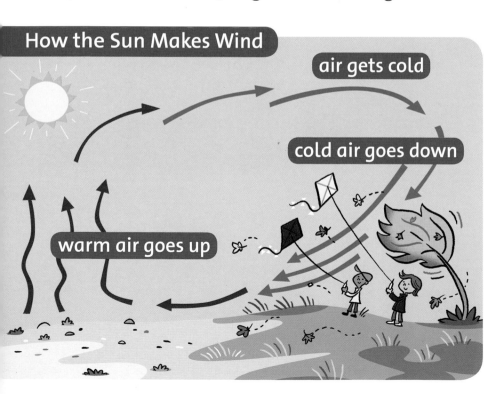

How the Sun Makes Wind

air gets cold

cold air goes down

warm air goes up

Flags in a Breeze

Wind blows. A breeze is wind that blows slowly. A breeze can blow flags in the sky. Some winds blow fast. A hurricane is wind that blows very fast. When there's a hurricane, people are scared. A hurricane can blow down trees and houses!

In a Hurricane

→ Go to pages 28–29 for activities.

6 Warm and Wet

the Tropics

In the Tropics, it's warm and wet all year. Many rainforests grow in the Tropics. In a rainforest, trees get lots of light and rain, and they grow very tall.

A Rainforest

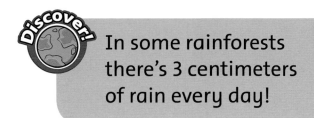 In some rainforests there's 3 centimeters of rain every day!

Many animals live in warm, wet rainforests. Monkeys live in trees and they eat nuts and fruit. Birds fly from tree to tree. Birds eat minibeasts. They eat nuts and fruit, too. Small frogs drink raindrops on the big leaves of rainforest trees.

A Rainforest Frog

→ Go to pages 30–31 for activities.

Cold and Dry

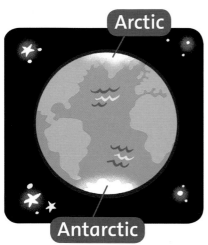

Arctic

Antarctic

In the Arctic and the Antarctic it's very cold and dry. A lot of the water is ice or snow. There are no trees – plants can't grow in these places. There's white ice and snow everywhere!

Snow and Ice in the Arctic

There aren't many animals in the Arctic and the Antarctic. There are no leaves, fruit, or nuts for animals to eat.

Seals swim in the ocean to find fish. They eat lots of fish and they get very fat. This helps them to be warm.

Seals

→ Go to pages 32–33 for activities.

8 People and Weather

Windows with Shutters

When it's sunny, people can get hot. Many buildings have windows with shutters. When it's sunny, the shutters stop the heat and light going in the buildings. Then people in the buildings don't get hot.

When it's sunny, many people wear a hat. Then their head doesn't get hot.

roof

Rain Falling off Roofs

When it's rainy, people can get wet. Buildings have roofs. The rain falls off the roofs and it doesn't go in the buildings. Then people in the buildings don't get wet.

When it's rainy, many people use an umbrella. Then they don't get wet.

What do you do when it's rainy and when it's sunny?

➔ Go to pages 34–35 for activities.

① Sunny

← Read pages 4–5.

1 **Find and write the words.**

a	y	r	e	s	i
l	i	b	t	n	y
d	b	s	u	n	y
u	l	i	g	h	t
s	r	t	w	e	k
g	c	h	e	a	t
e	a	r	t	h	z
p	i	z	u	l	n
h	e	a	r	n	s

1 <u>sun</u>   2 E_____

3 l_____   4 h_____

2 **Write *true* or *false*.**

1 The sun is a star.   <u>true</u>

2 The sun is very, very cold.   _____

3 Heat and light from the sun come
to Earth.   _____

4 The heat and light make Earth cold.   _____

3 **Complete the sentences.**

1 Some places are warm and ___sunny___
   all year.
2 Some places have _____ .
3 In summer, there's more light from the sun,
   so it's _____ .
4 In winter, there's less light from the sun,
   so it's _____ .

4 **Write the words.**

winter   cold   ~~warm~~   summer

1 ___warm___

3 _____

2 _____

4 _____

② Rainy

← Read pages 6–7.

1 Circle the correct words.

① cloud / river

② rain / cloud

③ river / ocean

④ ocean / sky

⑤ plants / animals

⑥ plants / animals

2 Write *true* or *false*.

1 Rain falls from the sun in the sky. _____

2 When big raindrops meet, they make one small raindrop. _____

3 When there are lots of big raindrops, rain falls to Earth. _____

4 People, plants, and animals use water to live and to grow. _____

3 Complete the sentences. Then write the numbers.

sky   oceans   clouds   rain   rivers   sunny

1 When rain falls, water goes into _____.

2 Water in rivers goes into _____.

3 When it's _____, water at the top of the ocean gets warm.

4 Some of the water goes up into the _____.

5 Water in the sky makes _____.

6 Then _____ falls again!

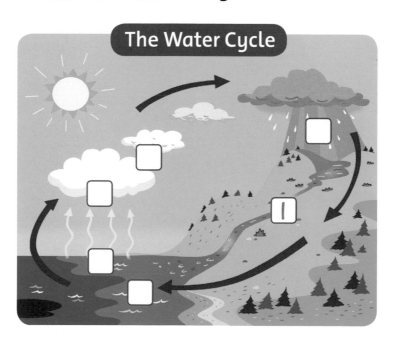
The Water Cycle

3 Cloudy

← Read pages 8–9.

1 Match. Then write the sentences.

Some clouds	many raindrops.
Some clouds are	have many raindrops.
Gray clouds have	are gray.
White clouds don't	white.

1 Some clouds are gray.

2 _____

3 _____

4 _____

2 Find and write the words.

skygraywhitesunhotlight

1 sky   3 _____   5 _____

2 _____   4 _____   6 _____

3 Complete the puzzle.
Then write the secret word.

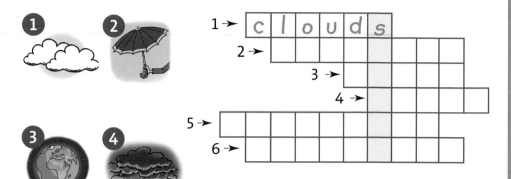

1 → | c | l | o | u | d | s |

2 →

3 →

4 →

5 →

6 →

The secret word is:

4 Circle the correct words.

1 Cumulonimbus clouds are very,
   very (big) / small.

2 Cumulonimbus clouds make
   big / small storms.

3 Cumulonimbus clouds
   stop / make lightning.

4 Lightning is very, very **hot** / cold.

4 Snowy

← Read pages 10–11.

1 Match.

1
When is water
in clouds ice?

It's snow.

2
What is ice when
it falls to Earth?

It's water.

3
What is snow
when it melts?

It goes into the
ground and rivers.

4
Where does
the water go?

When it's very
cold in the sky.

2 Number the sentences in order.

[ ] Then the snow is water again.

[ ] When ice falls to Earth, the ice is snow.

[ ] When snow falls on warm ground,
the snow melts.

[1] When it's very cold in the sky, water
in clouds is ice.

3 Write the words.

mountain   snow   house
cloud   skiing   car

1 _____   4 _____

2 _____   5 _____

3 _____   6 _____

4 Write *true* or *false*.

1 When snow falls on cold ground,
the snow melts.   _____

2 When snow falls on mountains,
people can't go skiing.   _____

3 When snow falls on streets, people
can't drive their cars.   _____

5 Windy

← Read pages 12–13.

1 Circle the correct words.

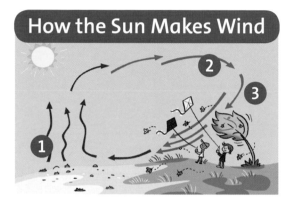

How the Sun Makes Wind

1 Warm air goes **up** / **down**.

2 Air gets **hot** / **cold**.

3 Cold air goes **up** / **down**.

2 Complete the sentences.

sky   cold   sun   down   air

1 In the sky there's _____ .

2 The _____ makes the air warm.

3 Warm air goes up into the _____ .

4 In the sky, the air gets _____ .

5 When the air is cold, it goes _____ again.

3 **Write the words.**

breeze house tree
sky hurricane flag

1 _____ 2 _____ 3 _____

4 _____ 5 _____ 6 _____

4 **Answer the questions.**

1 Which wind blows slowly?

A breeze blows slowly.

2 Which wind blows fast?

_____

3 What can a hurricane do?

_____

(6) Warm and Wet

← Read pages 14–15.

1 Write *true* or *false*.

1 In the Tropics, it's cold and dry. _____

2 Many rainforests grow in the Tropics. _____

3 In a rainforest, trees grow very small. _____

2 Find and write the words.

f	r	u	i	t	h	b	i	r	d	p
x	q	f	t	i	o	n	z	o	t	t
y	i	h	u	l	e	a	v	e	s	x
z	r	u	q	p	c	n	l	x	k	j
m	o	n	k	e	y	v	f	r	o	g
m	i	n	i	b	e	a	s	t	s	t

1 l _____

2 f _____

3 b _____

4 m _____

5 f _____

6 m _____

3 **Match. Then write the sentences.**

Many animals live in	nuts and fruit, too.
Monkeys eat nuts	raindrops on big leaves.
Birds eat minibeasts and	warm, wet rainforests.
Small frogs drink	and fruit.

1 _____

2 _____

3 _____

4 _____

4 **Answer the questions.**

1 When is it warm and wet in the Tropics?

_____

2 Where do monkeys live in a rainforest?

_____

3 What do birds do in a rainforest?

_____

7 Cold and Dry

← Read pages 16–17.

1 Complete the sentences.

| animals | snow | water |
| Arctic | ice | Antarctic | plants |

1 In the _____ and the _____ it's very cold and dry.

2 A lot of the _____ is ice or snow.

3 There are no trees – _____ can't grow in these places.

4 There's white _____ and _____ everywhere!

5 There aren't many _____ in the Arctic and the Antarctic.

2 Find and write the words.

oceannutsicesealfishtree

1 _____   3 _____   5 _____

2 _____   4 _____   6 _____

3 Circle the correct words.

1 Seals **walk** / **swim** in the ocean.

2 Seals eat **fish** / **fruit**.

3 Seals are **fat** / **thin**.

4 Seals are fat to help them to be **warm** / **cold**.

4 Answer the questions.

1 How do seals get very fat?

_____

2 What helps seals to be warm?

_____

8 People and Weather

← Read pages 18–19.

1 Match.

1 When it's sunny, people

2 When it's rainy, people

3 When it's sunny,

4 When it's rainy,

can get wet.

can get hot.

people use an umbrella.

people wear a hat.

2 Order the words.

1 have windows / Many buildings / with shutters.
   Many buildings have windows with shutters.

2 the heat and light / The shutters / stop / going in.

_____

3 people can get / When it's rainy, / wet.

_____

4 Rain / roofs. / falls off

_____

3 Complete the puzzle.

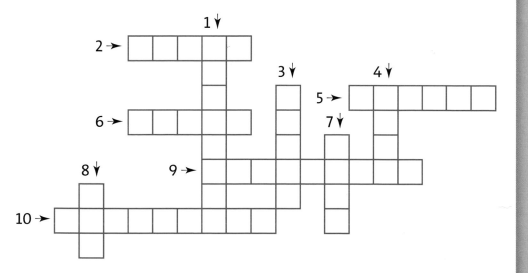

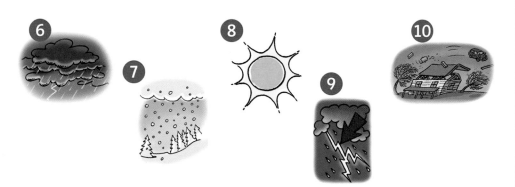

A Weather Diary

1 Complete the weather diary.

Monday		rainy all day gray clouds in the sky

Day	Draw the weather.	Write about the weather.
Monday		
Tuesday		
Wednesday		
Thursday		
Friday		
Saturday		
Sunday		

Project 2 Weather Cards

1 Complete the weather cards.

Place	Weather	Animals
The Antarctic	snow	seals

Place	Weather	Animals
Rainforests in the Tropics		

2 Write a weather card for where you live.

Place	Weather	Animals

37

Picture Dictionary

 blow

 buildings

 down

 dry

 Earth

 fall

 fast

 flag

 fruit

 ground

 grow

 heat

 ice

 leaves

 light

melt

minibeasts   minute   mountain   nuts

ocean   plants   raindrops   river

sky   slowly   storm   street

top   up   warm   wet

Oxford Read and Discover

Series Editor: Hazel Geatches • CLIL Adviser: John Clegg

Oxford Read and Discover graded readers are at six levels, for students from age 6 and older. They cover many topics within three subject areas, and support English across the curriculum, or Content and Language Integrated Learning (CLIL).

Available for each reader:
• Audio CD Pack (book & audio CD)
• Activity Book

Teaching notes & CLIL guidance: **www.oup.com/elt/teacher/readanddiscover**

Subject Area / Level	The World of Science & Technology	The Natural World	The World of Arts & Social Studies
1 300 headwords	• Eyes • Fruit • Trees • Wheels	• At the Beach • In the Sky • Wild Cats • Young Animals	• Art • Schools
2 450 headwords	• Electricity • Plastic • Sunny and Rainy • Your Body	• Camouflage • Earth • Farms • In the Mountains	• Cities • Jobs
3 600 headwords	• How We Make Products • Sound and Music • Super Structures • Your Five Senses	• Amazing Minibeasts • Animals in the Air • Life in Rainforests • Wonderful Water	• Festivals Around the World • Free Time Around the World
4 750 headwords	• All About Plants • How to Stay Healthy • Machines Then and Now • Why We Recycle	• All About Desert Life • All About Ocean Life • Animals at Night • Incredible Earth	• Animals in Art • Wonders of the Past
5 900 headwords	• Materials to Products • Medicine Then and Now • Transportation Then and Now • Wild Weather	• All About Islands • Animal Life Cycles • Exploring Our World • Great Migrations	• Homes Around the World • Our World in Art
6 1,050 headwords	• Cells and Microbes • Clothes Then and Now • Incredible Energy • Your Amazing Body	• All About Space • Caring for Our Planet • Earth Then and Now • Wonderful Ecosystems	• Food Around the World • Helping Around the World